MY CHRISTMAS

A Hide-and-Seek Story

By Sarah Reid Chisholm
Illustrated by Michelle Neavill

For my angel, Grace

MY CHRISTMAS ANGEL
A Hide-and-Seek Story

Copyright © 1993 Augsburg Fortress. All rights reserved. Except for brief quotations in critical articles or reviews, no part of this book may be reproduced in any manner without prior written permission from the publisher. Write to: Permissions, Augsburg Fortress, 426 S. Fifth St., Box 1209, Minneapolis, MN 55440

ISBN 0-8066-2601-1   LCCN 93-70323

Manufactured in the U.S.A.   AF 9-2601

97 96 95 94 1 2 3 4 5 6 7 8 9 10

"God will put his angels in charge of you to protect you wherever you go."
—Psalm 91:11 TEV

On Christmas Day last year, my grandma gave me a floppy angel doll. Its arms and legs moved any way I wanted them to.

This year, when Christmas was almost here, Daddy made up a game with my angel doll. "I'll hide it in a different place every day until Christmas," he said. "And you can find it."

The first day, he hid my angel in the kitchen. Mommy made Christmas cookies. They smelled yummy. They tasted yummy, too. I got to make one of my own with gooey frosting on it.

The next day I almost couldn't find my angel doll. That was the day I had to sit all by myself on a HARD chair for a LONG time because I called my brother a stupid frog.

He had to sit on a chair, too, because he pulled my hair.

My angel looked great on our Christmas tree. I could see it peeking through the branches.

When Auntie Ruth came over,
she brought me a red dress.
"My, how you've grown!" she said.

My angel doll sat near her
picture.

The day my brother was in the Christmas play, I didn't find my angel doll at all.

I felt sick from eating nine candy canes at the play. I fell asleep on the floor.

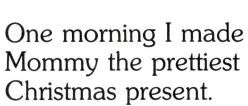

One morning I made Mommy the prettiest Christmas present.

My angel doll was watching me.

On Sunday we went to church and talked about Jesus' birthday. We sang Christmas songs. We learned that angels were there when Jesus was born. I wish I could have been there, too.

When Daddy hid my angel on a present, it took me a long time to find it because I had to shake all the presents first.

One time the angel doll was hiding in my toys.

That day we took a truck to give to a child who wasn't going to get any Christmas presents.

It was snowing one morning. I ran outside to catch snowflakes on my tongue. My best friend and I made a snowman. Daddy made sure my angel could watch me having fun.

On the very last day before Christmas, I couldn't find my angel until I looked

and looked.
I almost gave up.

Then my angel snuggled close to me as I went to sleep. Daddy tucked the blankets around me. "You're *my* angel," he said.

Daddy also told me that God sends angels to take care of me. I must be very special to God.

I wonder if God's angels look like mine?

THE END